1st Copy BOOK

for Advertising Copywriters & "Creative Writers"

MAXWELL OFORI NKRUMAH

SPECIAL

I dedicate this book to the Almighty God, who gives inspiration continuously through the Holy Spirit. To all you great Copywriters around the world, who contributed to an amazing discussion, which stimulated the birth of this book.

And to all my family members everywhere; I love you.

To my colleagues at Primus Advertising Ltd., Accra; you helped me discover my career-self.

Finally, to the Creative Team and Staff of Admedia DraftFCB, Accra; you're so inspirational!

CONTENTS

APPRECIATION

I do not know who to not include here; but surely, I cannot forget Mr. Adewale Adeoye-Famosa, CEO of Primus Advertising Ltd., Accra, who trained me as Copywriter; Mr. Emmanuel Addo, CEO of Admedia DraftFCB, Accra, whose personality, achievement and high expectations motivate me to do more; Ellie Jerow, Digital Information Specialist, Michigan, USA, whose belief and love for Social Media, inspired the writing of this book.

To all you great Creatives around the world whose contributions add to this awesome book, especially, Paul Dunwell, UK; Renato Bratkovic, Slovenia; LeAnn Wilson McGuire; North Carolina; Garret Donaldson, Orlando-Florida; Jan van der Reis, Mexico; Stacey Mathis, New York City; and Emily Suess, Indianapolis, Indiana. God bless you for supporting this course.

Kwasi Sarpong (Biggieman), Creative Executive, Global Media Alliance/Creative and Brands Manager, Silverbird Entertainment Ghana; your creative illustrations make this book richer and interesting. I wish I could also sing one of your beautiful songs here; you're a star. Thanks for involving the artistic touch of your cousin, Prince Kwabena Ofori. Your family is so endowed with the prowess of art. Gilbert Ofochu Apronti, the world can't wait to read your book! Lol! Mr. Lawrence Ntow Kwafo; your "Hero magazine" is changing lives, more than you ever imagined.

Mr. Emmanuel Kwame Dzakpasu, Creative Director at Admedia DraftFCB, Accra; there's something special and great about you. Lol! I love your belief in teamwork. And Mr. Ato Baiden, Account Director at Admedia DraftFCB, Accra; you're the definition of patience and multitasking.

May I salute these 4 super creative comrades: Samuel Ambasaki, Delali Seneadza, Gideon Agyeman, and Kwaku Duran Obeng; you guys are just phenomenal!

How can I forget about wonderful people like Mr. Edward Dapaah, Prophetess Abigail Asamoah, Pastor Gabriel Dela, Pastor Ralph Langdon, Mr. Kishore

Nankani, Mr. Alex Bannerman, Mr. Thomas Sowah, Mr. Dominic Ansah, Mr. Joseph Quashigah, Mr. Rexford Abutiate, Richard Anum, Mr. Agyeman Maxwell (Agyemax), Mr. Eugene Osei, Mr. Fosu K. Mensah, Mr. Thomas Sankara, Mr. Joseph Bonney, Mr. Daniel Mensah Sowah, Mr. Clement Nana Adu Koranteng, Mr. Sammy Anokye Kwakye, Rhoda Opoku, David Afiawo, Mr. Eric Koranteng, Miss Audrey Lamptey, Mrs. Tinawura Satuh, Mrs. Gifty Adu-Mensah, Emefa Nutor, Mr. Clive Okraku, Henrietta Mann, Mrs. Jenny Teiko Tetteh, Mr. Kofi Ansah, Prince Tabiri Addo, Edmund Kofi Ackom, Isaac Ahireng, Portia Adjei Frimpong, Linda Sowah, Raymond Kunle, Mr. Jackobus Neizer, Mr. Emmanuel Darko, Lopez Yamson, Kwame Oduro Koranteng, Daniel Teye, Mr. Bismark Tsevi, Mr. Bernard Acquah, Nii Odai, Grace Ketu, Mr. Julian Botwey, Mr. Dereck Gyimah, Patrick Yaw Kyeremateng, Reinhard Kyei-Baffour, Ellen Sakyi, Samuella Adjei, Rita Akosua Larbi, Woelinam Ahiabli, Jennifer Amansunu, Kafui Komlaga, Akosuah Safo, Zanita Coffie, Mr. Jerry Boansi, Serwaa Ansah-Sasraku, Jessica Sedem Agbanu, Jade Baah, Seth Mimaose, Frank Amenyo, Joseph Hamdaway, Bless Edeh, Mawuli Sachey and Anthony Awador - God Bless you!

Mr. Kweku Nyarko Eduful, the creative world, will forever remember your name, for typesetting this book so neatly.

Finally, to the indefatigable Creative and Digital Media Consultant at Admedia DraftFCB, Accra, Raphael Beecham, whose cover page design, inspires me to author more books.

INTRODUCTION

Hi Creatives!

David Ogilvy, popularly acclaimed as Father of modern Advertising, once indicated, that Copywriters are a silent people in ad agencies, but they are the most important.

Many people are not even aware of the existence of these crucial brains, behind most of the stunning advertising campaigns we see on Billboards, TV, the internet, or hear on Radio.

Some commercials on Radio and TV are so well thought out and crafted, that, when we listen or watch them, they challenge our own sense of imagination and creativity. Sometimes we marvel at how the "advert makers" were able to think so intelligently.

As a matter of fact, majority of astounding ad concepts are mostly found in the experienced markets of Europe, America, Asia and South Africa, where brands are well established. Also, in these markets, the ad agency business has existed for quite a long time.

Do you wonder how some people are able to create great ad concepts and campaigns? How do Copywriters and creative teams develop compelling ad concepts that make the world go **wow!?** They say the Chinese have a saying that, "if you want to hide something from an African, put it in books and he'll never find it, because he doesn't read". Could this be true? I'd rather believe that the fear of reading is a universal phobia. Ironically, all we need to know, in order to become the best in our chosen professions, can be found in certain books. Many experienced People have shared their rich experiences regarding best practices of their respective fields in several books.

A discussion with over 50 Creative professionals, most of who are accomplished Copywriters from different countries, about the best books to be recommended for aspiring Copywriters, stimulated the writing of this unique and powerful book. **It's just like asking so many experienced soldiers about which**

guns they preferred to use, and would recommend for aspiring warriors.

This discussion, which went on for many days, generated a fun-filled and exciting discourse. Occasionally, some writers highlighted their personal experiences, through anecdotes, which were amazingly deep and awesome.

In this book, you will discover which book(s) have influenced a lot of the world's best advertising creatives, especially, Copywriters and Creative Directors.

For the sake of those who are not conversant with the Advertising industry, especially "creative writers" and ordinary enthusiasts who may want to work in this exciting world, I will start off with informative chapters which would give a general overview on how ad agencies function, **with much emphasis on the Copywriter.**

Some people say digital communications is the future of Advertising and Marketing communications. Well, this book also uncovers powerful insights on Viral Advertising.

You have never found a book as informative, beneficial, and unique as this one. Congratulations, you are about to become the greatest creative person in the history of Advertising and Marketing Communications. You are the one!

The heart of creativity is discipline.
William (Bill) Bernbach

COPYWRITING VERSUS "CREATIVE WRITING"

1

Copywriting is creative writing for advertising. It is the art of writing skillfully and persuasively, to incite existing and potential customers, to purchase particular goods and services.

On the other hand, Creative writing involves every aspect of imaginative writing. It includes, Poetry writing, Fiction writing, Song writing, Screenwriting, Copywriting, and even Speech writing. Did you know that there was a profession called Speech Writing? The next time a public figure, especially a politician, wows you with a remarkable message, consider the possibility of a special speech craftsperson behind that message. Nevertheless, some rare public figures and politicians are gifted speechmakers.

Mathematically, Copywriting is a subset of creative writing. Lots of people are not even aware of a certain group of creative professionals called Copywriters.

Ironically the Copywriter's work is ubiquitous. It's all around you. On TV, Radio, Billboards, Posters; in Newspapers, Magazines, Brochures, Instruction Manuals, Flyers, and even on the Internet; you always see a Copywriter's work.

From the definition of Copywriting above, you can observe that the purpose of Copywriting, is, writing to persuade existing and prospective customers to purchase particular goods and services. You may agree with Ed Cox that, *"there are no creative or non-creative copywriters; only good ad-makers and bad"*.

Robert Bly states in his book, the Copywriter's Handbook, that, *a Copywriter is a salesperson behind a typewriter.* Robert credits one Judith K. Charles, for this remarkable definition. That's a great definition, because it enables amateur Copywriters to get wise early, in order to be successful in advertising. The earlier a Copywriter discovers that his/her main purpose is to persuade buyers, the faster he/she excels in the industry. It took me three (3) years to understand this simple fact!

Many junior Copywriters worry themselves with flowery words, and sometimes overstretched creativity, which may not cause customers to act. Such outstanding works may only entertain and win awards, rather than inciting target customers to act.

Modern customers are so wild because of overexposure; it takes a successful copywriter to **"catch them, and tame them."** This involves writing with the consumer insight, in order to incite.

Make it simple. Make it memorable.
Make it inviting to look at. Make it fun to read.

Leo Burnett

The definition on the tree above, as stated by another writer, is very interesting. **Copywriting is verbal carpentry**. So simple and lovely. But when I grew in the industry, I realized that if my work was to be based on the foundation of this definition of "verbal carpentry", I would not excel as Copywriter.

Yes, the work involves verbal carpentry; but it requires verbal persuasion. If not, your output will be like a carpenter who has joined pieces of wood to form an object which cannot be classified as furniture. And since customers are unable to determine its usefulness for them, they don't buy it. But if customers could see a chair or a table created out of the joinery of those pieces of wood, they might buy it.

Also, if the chair had an additional benefit of massaging, its sale would even be faster. So it is with Copywriting. You join words to form images that cause people to buy. And if your words spell out additional unique benefits for your customers, the better the chances of urging them to buy.

Every Copywriter must note two (2) important facts:

Firstly; know that you are a creative writer.
Secondly, your work must lead to customer demand.

I prefer to use the phrase, **customer demand,** instead of sale; because sale is someone else's job. You only drive customers to make it (the sale) happen. Therefore, if you write a compelling copy, making customers troop to buy from a dealer, where a lazy or rude salesperson, or a customer service attendant drives them away; you are not to blame. Your success as Copywriter here, is, that you were able to make customers troop to the dealers. However, Victor Schwab disagrees. He believes a good copy is all that matters.

"Poor copy cannot overcome faults or gaps in dealer distribution; it cannot even cash in on the finest dealer setups. But good copy can, and does, surmount many dealer difficulties, making them secondary, and selling in spite of them."

Victor Schwab

DO YOU WANT TO WORK IN ADVERTISING?

2

The simple organogram below summarizes the basic structure of an advertising agency:

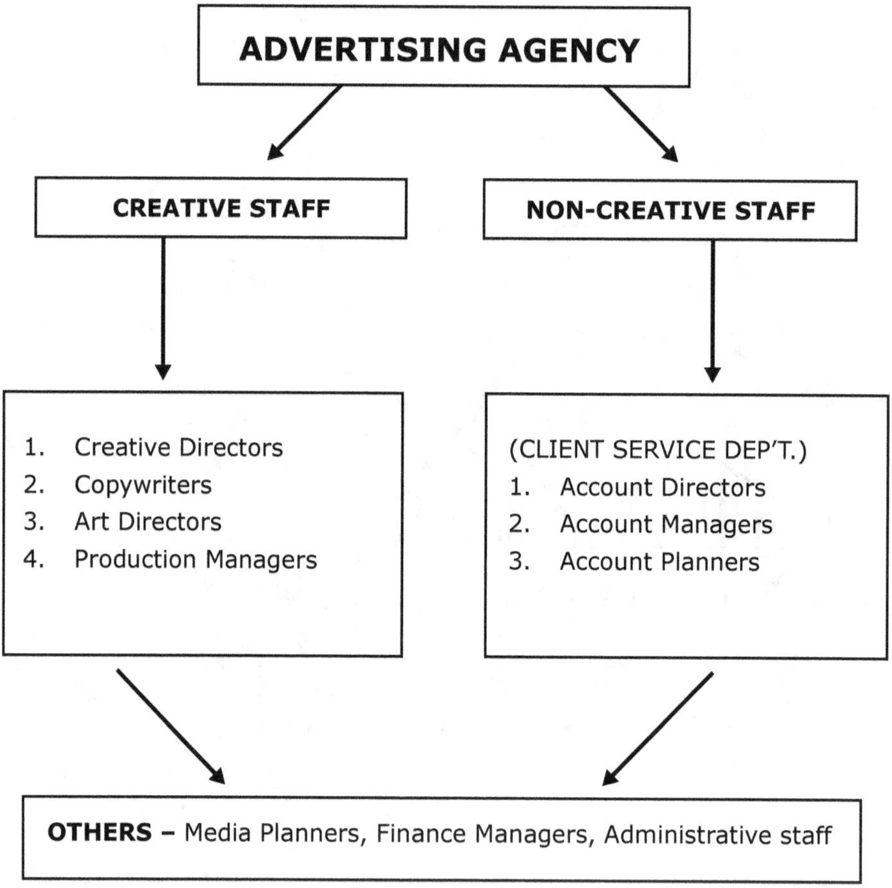

```
                    ┌─────────────────────────┐
                    │   ADVERTISING AGENCY    │
                    └─────────────────────────┘
              ┌──────────────┴──────────────┐
              ▼                              ▼
    ┌──────────────────┐          ┌──────────────────────┐
    │  CREATIVE STAFF  │          │  NON-CREATIVE STAFF  │
    └──────────────────┘          └──────────────────────┘
```

CREATIVE STAFF	NON-CREATIVE STAFF
1. Creative Directors	(CLIENT SERVICE DEP'T.)
2. Copywriters	1. Account Directors
3. Art Directors	2. Account Managers
4. Production Managers	3. Account Planners

OTHERS – Media Planners, Finance Managers, Administrative staff

In ad agency terms, clients are called Accounts. Therefore, an agency which works for Ford motors is said to be working on the Ford Account.

The Account Manager is assigned to manage specific Accounts in an ad agency. He/she is the liaison officer between the client and the agency. The **Account Director,** being a top or senior Account Manager, supervises various Account Managers in the client service department of the agency. In other words, various Account Managers report to an Account Director.

Before an agency proceeds to work on a particular advertising campaign, a client sends a **brief** to the agency, through the respective Account Manager. A brief is the job instruction for the agency, with regards to a required advertising work.

There are two (2) kinds of briefs in ad agency terms. These are the **Advertising brief,** and the **Creative brief.** The only difference is that the Advertising brief is written by the client for the agency; whereas the Creative brief is written by an Account Manager for the agency. The creative brief may either be a translation of an Advertising brief by the Account Manager, or completely written by the Account Manager. The brief spells out the direction an advertising campaign must follow. Like the architectural blueprint to the builder, so is the brief to the ad maker.

Account Planners are research personnel, responsible for providing additional consumer/target market information for the agency, in order to create impactful campaigns. Just as an Account Manager is the client's rep in the agency; an Account Planner is the consumer's rep in the agency. Account Planners enable the agency, especially, the creative team, to understand the mind of the consumer.

Advertising is Salesmanship in Print.

John E. Kennedy

THE CREATIVE TEAM

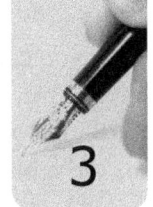

3

From the organogram in the previous chapter, the creative team consists of the Creative Director(s), the Copywriter(s), the Art Director(s) and the Production Manager(s).

The Creative Director

He/She is the leader of the creative team in an ad agency. A Creative Director in Advertising, is, an accomplished Copywriter or Art Director, with the clout to evaluate both copy (text) and image (art) in a compelling way.

The Copywriter

The Copywriter is the conceptualizer or ideas person of an ad agency. Basically, he/she does the following:

* Helps to develop the creative strategy/big idea for ad campaigns

* Writes the copy (text) and suggests appropriate images for press and outdoor advertisements.

* Develops concepts for TV commercials and documentaries

* Collaborates with other members of the creative team to audition for the appropriate casts in TV commercials

* Liaises with Film directors to direct TV commercials

* Develops concepts and scripts for Radio commercials

* Selects the appropriate voice over artistes and directs them in recording studios to produce radio commercials

* Develops viral video Ad campaigns for the internet

If you can perform the tasks above, you can be a successful Copywriter.

Brainstorming is a great resource for the Copywriter. It is an effective part of the creative process, as you will soon discover in this book. The best way to answer a brief is to find the best Creative Strategy or Big Idea. Big ideas are generally the result of a proper brainstorming session. *It is said that, unless your advertising contains a big idea, it will pass like a ship in the night.*

The Creative strategy/Big Idea is the creative springboard on which all ideas for a particular ad campaign are derived.
To succeed as Copywriter, you need to think deeply before you write. It doesn't mean that your ideas must be complex. The best ideas are simple, and easily understood by everyone.

The Art Director is the artist partner of the Copywriter in a creative department. He/she is in charge of creating the pictorial impressions of the Copywriter's words or copy. An Art Director's art is either based on the Copywriter's pictorial suggestions or his/her own artistic impressions of the copywriter's texts/copy. The illustrations in this book are the results of a Copywriter and Art Director collaboration.

The Production Manager
The Production Manager liaises with production houses, such as printing presses, recording studios, as well as TV production houses, ensuring that respective agency assignments are executed successfully. However, with Audio/ Visual production (TV and Radio), he collaborates with the Copywriter to assist in directing.

Unless your advertising contains a big idea,
it will pass like a ship in the night

David Ogilvy

A LETTER FROM DAVID OGILVY

4

In 1948, UK born David Ogilvy, acclaimed as the father of modern advertising, founded the Ogilvy and Mather group in New York, USA; a company he built to become one of the largest advertising networks in the world. Ogilvy was a college dropout, a chef, a door-to-door salesman, who finally became one of the world's ever greatest Copywriters.

A letter he wrote in 1955 to one Mr. Ray Calt, gives a list of **12 incredible insights** into his habits as Copywriter. From refusing to use a typewriter, to growling at his wife, to downing a half-bottle of rum if uninspired; David Ogilvy's letter is rife with colourful tips of insight into the world of a Copywriter. But please, don't force yourself to adopt his habits. Just be you.

April 19, 1955

Dear Mr. Calt,

On March 22nd you wrote to me asking for some notes on my work habits as a Copywriter. They are appalling, as you are about to see:

1. I have never written an advertisement in the office. Too many interruptions. I do all my writing at home.

2. I spend a long time studying the precedents. I look at every advertisement which has appeared for competing products during the past 20 years.

3. I am helpless without research material—and the more "motivational" the better.

4. I write out a definition of the problem and a statement of the purpose which I wish the campaign to achieve. Then I go no further until the statement and its principles have been accepted by the client.

5. Before actually writing the copy, I write down every conceivable fact and selling idea. Then I get them organized and relate them to research and the *copy platform.*

6. Then I write the headline. As a matter of fact I try to write 20 alternative headlines for every advertisement. And I never select the final headline without asking the opinion of other people in the agency. In some cases I seek the help of the **research department** and get them to do a split-run on a battery of headlines.

7. At this point I can no longer postpone the actual copy. So I go home and sit down at my desk. I find myself entirely without ideas. I get bad-tempered. If my wife comes into the room I growl at her. (This has gotten worse since I gave up smoking.)

8. I am terrified of producing a lousy advertisement. This causes me to throw away the first 20 attempts.

9. If all else fails, I drink half a bottle of rum and play a Handel oratorio on the gramophone. This generally produces an uncontrollable gush of copy.

10. The next morning I get up early and edit the gush.

11. Then I take the train to New York and my secretary types a draft. (I cannot type, which is very inconvenient.)

12. I am a lousy Copywriter, but I am a good editor. So I go to work editing my own draft. After four or five editings, it looks good enough to show to the client. If the client changes the copy, I get angry — because I took a lot of trouble writing it, and what I wrote I wrote on purpose.

Altogether it is a slow and laborious business. I understand that some Copywriters have much greater facility.

Yours sincerely,
D.O.

If it doesn't sell, it isn't creative
David Ogilvy

THE COPY PLATFORM

5

One particular phrase is worthy of note in the 5th point of David Ogilvy's letter in chapter 4:

5. Before actually writing the copy, I write down every conceivable fact and selling idea. Then I get them organized and relate them to research and the <u>*copy platform.*</u>

An often overlooked document which bears great importance on successful Copywriting is the Copy platform. The Copy platform, also called the **Copy strategy,** is, a Plan for use by the Copywriter that defines the basic theme of the advertising campaign, and serves as a guide for writing an advertisement. It is a situation analysis where you look at your market, specific audience, client's objectives and the stage in the development and life of the product, service, or brand that you are preparing to advertise.

The development of a Copy platform is a collaborative effort between a client and an agency. A copy platform enables both Agency and Client to have the same direction toward the development of a **Creative Strategy/Big Idea.** Sometimes an agency presents a Copy platform in a proposal to client; giving the client an idea of the creative work to be done, before developing the Big Idea and the advertisement. However, I once tried this approach with a client in Ghana, but it failed. He just couldn't wait for me to get the final copy done for him. You know, some clients only ask, *"what is the concept?"* instead of *"what is the process?".*

The Copy Platform forms the basis for creating consistent brand communications for all media.
It covers the product's features/benefits, competitive advantages/weaknesses, information about the target audience, the tone of the message, and the Unique Selling Proposition (USP).

Different agencies have unique approaches to developing Copy platforms. Some agencies differentiate the **Creative brief** from the **Copy platform,** whilst others classify both as same.

Here, let's differentiate a Creative brief from a Copy platform. A Creative brief may be prepared from a Copy platform. Compared to the Copy platform, the Creative brief describes a more linear progression; from where you are to where you want to be and how you will get there. Therefore, the **creative strategy** is more defined in a creative brief than in most Copy platforms.

SUMMARY

Copy Platform	Creative Brief
1. Covers the product's features/ benefits, competitive advantages/ weaknesses, information about the target audience, the tone of the message, and a simple, overriding statement about the product or the USP.	1. Describes a more linear progression, from where you are to where you want to be and how you will get there.
2. Examines a marketing problem.	2. Provides a creative solution plan for the marketing problem.

The consumer tends to remember just one thing from advertising – one strong claim, or one strong concept.

Rosser Reeves

Now let's take a look at samples of Copy platforms and Creative briefs:

COPY PLATFORM 1 (Visit Florida)
By Lynn Maikke

(1) Basic problem or issue the advertising must address
- Psychographic trend toward decreasing repeat visitation or increased intervals between visits to Florida as a result of attractive alternatives
- Shift from long vacations to short vacations

(2) Advertising and Communications objectives
- Increase interest and awareness in taking a Florida vacation
- Increase domestic leisure tourism from out-of-state residents as measured by an increase in net leisure nights of paid lodging (i.e. decreasing the "gap").
- Increasing rental car usage is a secondary objective ($2/day surcharge).
- The goal common to all communications challenge is to convey that VISIT FLORIDA is the official tourism marketing organisation for Florida.

(3) Target audience
- Persons who do not live in Florida, travel at least 100 miles one-way to the state, and spend at least one night in paid lodging.
- Minority marketing must be included.
- Acquire new customers who have not been to Florida on vacation before, or not in more than three years, or persuade current customers to consume the product more frequently.

(4) Major selling idea or key benefits to communicate
- The strongest single selling point is the diversity of the product.
- Communicate the beauty, fantasy, and fun of Florida.
- Emphasize the importance of pampering on a vacation, along with the importance taking multiple vacations each year.
- Emphasize the three bodies of water, including the Atlantic, Carribean, and Gulf of Mexico.
- The dominant travel motivators include the climate, waterside activities, and culture-based activities.
- Note: The heritage of the product is a two-edged sword for Florida

because it has to be positioned as both established and new again.

(5) Creative Strategy (i.e. campaign theme, appeal, executive technique).
- Illustrate the diversity of Florida through visual and verbal metaphors regarding the beauty, fantasy, and fun of Florida.
- Use appealing visual images of the sunny climate, oceans fronts, nature, sporting activities, theme parks, and culture.
- Execute via an umbrella multi-media technique.

(6) Supporting information and requirements.
- Avoid advertisements that overtly extol the virtues of staying in hotels and motels.
- Market the entire state.
- Do not show preferences to any branded products within the state.

COPY PLATFORM 2
Product: Easy Bath

Advertising Objective:
The objective of this campaign is to introduce **Easy Bath,** a portable bathhouse unit, as the bathing solution product for Ghanaians living in compound houses.

Target Audience
People living in compound houses, who do not enjoy the luxury and comfort of a self contained room with its own bathroom. Mathematically, we are considering about 70% of Ghanaians.

Customer Benefit
Customers of easy bath will enjoy the luxury and comfort of using their own bathhouse with their family.

Supporting Selling Point(s):
- Easy Bath is portable - it can be used in or outside the room, at customer's own convenience.

- Since easy bath is targeted at the popular market, i.e. about 70% of Ghanaians living in compound houses, who share limited bathrooms with several other families, it is low priced.

Creative Strategy (i.e. campaign theme, appeal, execution technique)
- Advertising must be testimonial, demonstrating the satisfaction in various users of the product.

- Advertising must convey comfort, simplicity and a touch of good-natured humour

People aren't interested in you.
They're interested in themselves.

Dale Carnegie

The questionnaire below will help you generate effective creative briefs:

- What do we want to accomplish? (Objective)
- Who are we talking to) (Target audience)
- What do they think now (Current position)
- What do we want them to think? (Reinforce position and reposition)
- Why should they think this? (Features/Benefits)
- What is our message? (How do we say it and show it/what is the one thing)

Sample Creative Brief

Client: Veromn Partners
Product: Easy Bath

What do we want to accomplish?
The objective of this campaign is to introduce Easy Bath, a portable bathroom set, as the bathing solution product for Ghanaians living in compound houses.

Who are we talking to?
People living in congested compound houses, who do not enjoy the luxury and comfort of a self contained room having its own bathroom. Mathematically, we are talking to about 70% of Ghanaians.

What do they think now?
They prefer to live in houses which are rather self-contained with their inbuilt bathrooms. Most of them are not comfortable to live in houses where they join long queues to wait for their turns to bath, every morning.
Also, some are not comfortable with sharing bathrooms with other families.

What do we want them to think?
To make our target know, that, they do not have to live in expensive self contained houses in order to enjoy the luxury of having their own bathrooms. We want them to see Easy bath as the best solution to owning their own bathrooms in any house they may be living in, whether in a village without electricity, or in the urban areas.

Why should they think this?
Easy bath will be positioned as a purely hygienic product which provides the comfort of living in one's own apartment/house with an inbuilt bathroom. Easy bath is affordable

and can therefore be purchased by anyone who does not have the ability to rent an expensive self contained apartment.

What is our message?
Easy bath is your solution for owning a portable bathroom at a low cost everyone can afford.

Consumer Profile

The consumer profile shows a "close up" of the target consumer of a proposed campaign. This profile takes the copy platform or the creative brief a step further. Who is this consumer? Where does he live? Where does he hangout? Where does he work? What are his hobbies? What TV and radio programmes does he watch? What are his aspirations? These questions, and more, will help you zoom in on your target consumer. When you are able to define him/her this way, you are in the position to create an impactful campaign.

Consumer Profile for "Easy Bath"

Meet Kwame Agyei
Kwame Agyei, a 40 year old primary school teacher, lives with his wife, Ameley, a petty trader and their 3 children in a chamber and hall room within a large compound house in Accra.

They do not have their own bathroom and kitchen. The family uses their porch as kitchen and shares 2 central bathhouses with other 30 co-tenants.

One of the problems they face every morning, is, joining long queues to wait for their turns to bath. This often results to Kwame Agyei turning up late for work; and his children also going to school late.

Kwame prefers to build or rent a self contained house for his growing family, but, his current earnings of less than $500 monthly does not enable him to enjoy that comfort in Accra.

To solve the problem of sharing limited number of bathrooms with numerous co-tenants, "Easy Bath", a portable bathhouse unit, which can be used within any appropriate space, i.e. inside, in-front or behind one's room, is an ideal product for Kwame's family.

*I don't know how to speak to everybody,
only to somebody.*

Howard Gossages

BRAINSTORMING

6

Brainstorming is a vital element of successful Copywriting. **In an ad agency, Brainstorming** usually involves a team of Creatives and Account Executives/ Managers meeting to freely think, and develop ideas, aimed at killing a Marketing Communications task.

I once worked in an agency where group brainstorming was the most annoying experience for me as Copywriter. In these painful sessions, I found certain people who would never suggest any idea, but were always the first to smash your idea as soon as you let it out. They are the first to point out why an idea will not work. These people would always see the *"why it won't work"* instead of the *"why and how it can/may work"*.

The fact is that, when an idea first pops up in the brain, it is sometimes funny, and unintelligent. At group brainstorming sessions, people may say their ideas just as they popped up in their brains. It is by courtesy of all present to receive, polish the idea together, and analyze its viability, before deciding on the fate of that idea with respect to the creative brief.

As the saying goes, "there's wisdom in every foolish talk". It means, certain perceived "foolish talks" at brainstorming sessions, may be the seeds of great and impactful campaigns. *"The best ideas often come as jokes".*

However, this does not warrant anybody to attend a brainstorming session to speak gibberish. Express your ideas with regards to the brief. But still, feel free to think in all angles. Those who kill ideas, are not healthy elements in any successful group brainstorming session.

To have a great idea, have a lot of them.
Thomas A. Edison

Another reason why I hated group brainstorming, is that, I think very well when I'm alone than when thinking together with a group. In solitude, I am a great thinker. There was also a latent phobia, that, probably, the chosen idea at a brainstorming session might come from someone other than me the Copywriter. I feared that since the idea didn't come from me, I might not be able to create effective concepts out of them. I was damn wrong!

Brainstorming is actually a great resource for every Copywriter. You don't have to worry as a Copywriter, when an Account Executive suggests during a brainstorming session, that, *"the TVC should be a narration of a kid, praising his mum"*. He has done about 20% of the work for you. It means that you do not have to torture your brain again, trying to think about appropriate scenarios to suit the agreed creative strategy/big idea. Once the scenario has been created, you have to employ your artistic skill to paint it so well.

If a "non-creative" person, or even a client, suggests a scenario for Radio or TVC, it doesn't mean he/she can do the script the way you (Copywriter) would get it done. For instance, when you suggest to a painter that you want **a blue monkey ridding a pink bicycle** to be drawn on a canvass, it doesn't mean that you too can paint that picture on canvass.

At a group brainstorming session, the best idea must not necessarily come from the Copywriter. He/She must contribute freely and positively to all manner of ideas that may arise. The big assurance, is, that at the end of a proper brainstorming session, great ideas will be developed. And from there, he/she can paint awesome pictures with his/her touch of creativity as Copywriter. Group brainstorming is so useful!

A BRIEF HISTORY OF BRAINSTORMING

As the popular saying goes, if you don't know where you are coming from, you don't know where you're going. Therefore, knowledge of the source of "brainstorming" will help us appreciate the subject best.

In 1941, a team led by BBDO's advertising executive, Alex Osborn, coined the term "brainstorm". In his famous book, 'your creative power', Alex Osborn explained that, to brainstorm, "means, using the *brain* to *storm* a creative problem and to do so in commando fashion, each stormer audaciously attacking the same objective."

Osborn found that conventional business meetings were inhibiting the creation of new ideas and proposed some rules designed to help stimulate them.

He was looking for rules which would give people the freedom of mind and action to spark off and reveal new ideas. To **"think up"** was originally the term he used to describe the process he developed, and that in turn came to be known as "brainstorming".

To achieve great results, Osborn came out with the following rules for proper brainstorming:

- **N o criticism of ideas**
- **Go for large quantities of ideas**
- **Build on each other's ideas**
- **Encourage wild and exaggerated ideas**

He found that when these rules were followed, a lot more ideas were created, and that a greater quantity of original ideas gave rise to a greater quantity of useful ideas. He believed that **quantity produced quality.**

Using these new rules, people's natural inhibitions were reduced; inhibitions which prevented them from putting forward ideas which they felt might be considered "wrong" or "stupid". Osborn also found generating "silly" ideas could spark off very useful ideas because they changed the way people thought.

The development of this original technique was revolutionary and has since changed our world. With increasing refinement of process, and the introduction of creative thinking techniques, the world of easy idea generation is yours for the taking. You need never be stuck for a new idea, whether you are in a group or working by yourself.

Imagination is one of the last remaining legal means you have to gain an unfair advantage over your competition.

Ed McCabe

1st Copy BOOK for Advertising Copywriters & "Creative Writers"

MODERN BRAINSTORMING TECHNIQUES (source:wikipedia.com)

Nominal Group Technique
- Participants are asked to write their ideas anonymously.
- A facilitator collects the ideas and the group votes on each idea. This process is called distillation.
- After distillation, the top ranked ideas may be sent back to the group or to subgroups for further brainstorming.
- For example, one group may work on the colour required in a product. Another group may work on the size, and so forth.
- Each group will come back to the whole group for ranking the listed ideas.
- Sometimes ideas that were previously dropped may be brought forward again once the group has re-evaluated the ideas.

Group Passing Technique
- Each person in a circular group writes down one idea, and then passes the piece of paper to the next person, who adds some thoughts.
- This continues until everybody gets his or her original piece of paper back. By this time, it is likely that the group will have extensively elaborated on each idea.
- The group may also create an "idea book" and post a distribution list or routing slip to the front of the book. On the first page is a description of the problem.
- The first person to receive the book lists his or her ideas and then passes the book to the next person on the distribution list.
- The second person can log new ideas or add to the ideas of the previous person. This continues until the distribution list is exhausted.
- A follow-up "read out" meeting is then held to discuss the ideas logged in the book. This technique takes longer, but it allows individuals time to think deeply about the problem.

Team Idea Mapping Method
- This method of brainstorming works by the method of association.
- The process begins with a well-defined topic.
- Each participant brainstorms individually, then all the ideas are merged onto one large idea map.
- During this consolidation phase, participants may discover a common

understanding of the issues as they share the meanings behind their ideas.
- During this sharing, new ideas may arise by the association, and they are added to the map as well.
- Once all the ideas are captured, the group can prioritize and/or take action.

Electronic Brainstorming
- It is a computerized version of the manual brainstorming technique typically supported by an electronic meeting system (EMS) such as email, electronic chat rooms, social media or peer-to-peer software.
- Ideas are entered independently. Contributions become immediately visible to all and are typically anonymized to encourage openness and reduce personal prejudice.
- Since all are exposed to everyone's idea, attention is focused by the group members on these ideas and this attention has been proposed to cognitively stimulate the brainstormer.
- During an EBS session, participants have control over their activity and can attend to the ideas of others while also creating their own, continually exposing participants to a flow of ideas.
- EBS techniques have been shown to produce more ideas and help individuals focus their attention on the ideas of others better than a brainwriting technique (where participants write individual written notes in silence and then subsequently communicate them with the group).
- EBS enables much larger groups to brainstorm on a topic than would normally be productive in a traditional brainstorming session.

Directed Brainstorming
- Directed brainstorming is a variation of electronic brainstorming (described above), conducted manually or with computers.
- Directed brainstorming works when the solution space (that is, the set of criteria for evaluating a good idea) is known prior to the session. If known, those criteria can be used to constrain the Ideation process intentionally.
- In directed brainstorming, each participant is given one sheet of paper (or electronic form) and told the brainstorming question.
- They are asked to produce one response and stop; then all of the papers (or forms) are randomly swapped among the participants.
- The participants are asked to look at the idea they received and to create a new idea that improves on that idea based on the initial criteria.

- The forms are then swapped again and respondents are asked to improve upon the ideas, and the process is repeated for three or more rounds.
- In the laboratory, directed brainstorming has been found to almost triple the productivity of groups over electronic brainstorming.

"Logic will get you from A to Z; imagination will get you everywhere."

Albert Einstein

Logic

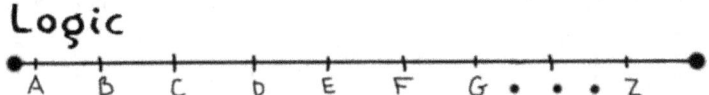

Imagination

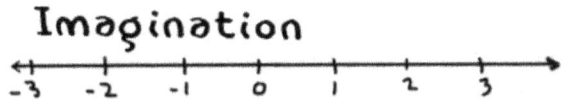

QUESTION BRAINSTORMING

- This technique is also called "Questorming".
- The process involves brainstorming the, rather than trying to come up with immediate answers and short term solutions.
- Theoretically, this technique should not inhibit participation as there is no need to provide solutions.
- The answers to the questions form the framework for constructing future action plans.
- Once the list of questions is set, it may be necessary to prioritize them to reach to the best solution in an orderly way.

GUIDED BRAINSTORMING

- A guided brainstorming session is time set aside to brainstorm either individually or as a collective group about a particular subject under the constraints of perspective and time.
- This type of brainstorming removes all cause for conflict and constrains conversations while stimulating critical and creative thinking in an engaging, balanced environment. Innovative ideas consistently emerge.
- Participants are asked to adopt different mindsets for pre-defined period of time while contributing their ideas to a central mind map drawn by a pre-appointed scribe.
- Having examined a multi-perspective point of view, participants seemingly see the simple solutions that collectively create greater growth. Action is assigned individually.
- Following a guided brainstorming session participants emerge with ideas ranked for further brainstorming, research and questions remaining unanswered and a prioritized, assigned, actionable list that leaves everyone with a clear understanding of what needs to happen next and the ability to visualize the combined future focus and greater goals of the group.

INDIVIDUAL BRAINSTORMING

- "Individual brainstorming" is the use of brainstorming in solitude.
- It typically includes such techniques as free writing, free speaking, word association, and drawing a mind map, which is a visual note taking technique in which people diagram their thoughts.
- Individual brainstorming is a useful method in creative writing. Some people believe that it is superior to traditional group brainstorming.

"Reality can be beaten with enough imagination."

Mark Twain

WHAT KIND OF DISCUSSION TYPE ARE YOU?

People often reveal their character in their approach to discussions. The abbreviation AI stands for **Appreciative Inquiry;** a method attributed to the American management expert, David Cooperrider, which involves **concentrating on the strengths, positive attributes and potential of a company or a person, rather than weaknesses.** 'What is going really well at the moment?' replaces the classic question 'What is the problem?' Concentrating on weakness creates a negative impression.

Every person, every system, every product, every idea has faults. In the best-case scenario, an awareness of this fact can lead to a determined pursuit of perfection. But in many cases, focusing too strongly on the flaws of an idea or project stifles the open and positive approach that is essential for good working practices. The basic principle is to take an idea that is not yet fully developed and to continue developing it, instead of prematurely abandoning it.

You are likely to meet four (4) kinds of discussants at a brainstorming session. These can be identified by the way they react to your suggestions:

- **The fault-finder:** 'The idea is good, but...'
- **The dictator:** 'No!'
- **The schoolteacher:** 'No, the idea isn't good because...'
- **The AI thinker:** 'Yes, and we could also...'

Any fool can criticize. And most fools do.

Benjamin Franklin

VIRAL MARKETING/ "VIRATISING"

7

Viral marketing, which I call, **"Viratising"**, is a digital marketing strategy which thrives on the power of word-of-mouth, to advertise products and services. The concept is rooted in the idea, that, word-of-mouth is the most effective form of advertising. You probably trust recommendations from your friends and other people than recommendations from TV and Radio commercials.

. The advent of the internet, plus its associated myriad of social media platforms, has endorsed word-of-mouth, and thus viral marketing, as a powerful modern form of advertising. People are close to people than ads are, to people. The theory of **"Six degrees of separation",** first proposed in 1929 by Frigyes Karinthy, indicates that, there are at most 5 acquaintances/intermediaries between any two individuals on earth.

An idea is said to have gone viral when as a result of its relevance, wit or humour, it incites or urges people to share with other people – via Social Media sites, WhatsApp, SMS etc.

Many vibrant companies are now exploring the advantages of this new horizon of "Viratising". It is actually cost effective (almost FREE), compared to traditional advertising. With "Viratising", you don't spend on expensive media buying. All you do, is, post your viral content (Video, Audio, Image, or Text) on any Social Media site; and almost magically, communities of people get compelled to pass it on to their friends. Before you realize, the whole world knows about your idea or brand.

When Cindy Gordon, vice president of new media and marketing partnerships at Universal Orlando Resort was charged with launching "The Wizarding World of Harry Potter", she didn't engage the old rules of marketing. She rather told only 7 people about the new attraction, whilst these 7 people told tens of thousands. The mainstream media listened to those tens of thousands and wrote about the news in their newspapers and magazine articles, in TV and radio reports, and in blog posts. Gordon's strategy **"Earned media"** for Free. She estimates that

350 million people around the world heard the news that Universal Resort was creating the Wizarding world of Harry Potter theme park.

Here's a piece of viral marketing advice from Cindy Gordon:

> *"Nimble companies are using the Web in ways that they could never do before. New media has created a new marketing environment where the old rules of marketing no longer apply. When you have a passionate fan base for your brand, the Internet is especially vital for going viral. Communicating to a small but powerful group of fans first online to enlist their support is a smart way to ensure positive coverage in the mainstream press. The power of the Internet makes it easier for people to fall in love with you faster. But beware—it also makes it easier for them to fall out of love with you faster. It's a double-edged sword. Listen constantly to what's being said about you. Social media technologies do not make a brand viral; they merely allow consumers to tell others about good brands. The main thing is to be different and relevant with your brand. And when you have that, the sheer power of the Internet can accelerate your brand. Traditional media takes weeks to build brand awareness and months to build preference. The Internet can make your brand famous literally overnight".*

He who wants to persuade should put his trust not in the right argument, but in the right word.

Joseph Conrad

"VIRATISING" STRATEGIES

Strategy 1

In his book, Contagious – Why things catch on, Professor Jonah Berger shares six (6) research based principles, abbreviated as "STEPPS", which guarantees that an idea goes viral:

- <u>S</u>ocial Currency
- <u>T</u>riggers
- <u>E</u>motion
- <u>P</u>ublic
- <u>P</u>ractical Value
- <u>S</u>tories

Social Currency

Social currency is the idea, that, what we talk about influences how people see us. So just like the cloths we wear and the cars we drive, the things we say influences whether people think we're cool and interesting or dumb and boring; whether we're smart in the know or not really someone they'll like to talk to. What we say are a kind of currency; they influence whether or not people would like to invite us to parties or whether or not we're going to be invited back to that second date. For something to be remarkable, it means that it is worthy of remark – whether it is surprising, interesting or novel. Things are remarkable because they violated expectations.

Social currency explores the idea of **status by association;** where people feel they belong to a higher social class, or that they are smarter, through knowledge of new music, actor, movie, restaurant, resort, club or access to secret info. A brand can ride on Social currency to go viral.

When Reggie Rockstone (originator Ghana's hiplife music genre) opened his club, **Rockstone's Office,** in Accra, people who first visited the place felt so proud and cool. I remember a friend of mine showing me a stamp of Rockstone's office in his palm, which he had kept from his previous night's visit to the club. Man, he was proud to show me that he had been to Rockstone's office!

Triggers

This explores the idea, that, when something is **top-of-mind,** it becomes **tip-of-tongue.** Coca cola have tried to exploit this idea in Ghana by bonding the beverage with certain traditional foods in a campaign. The rationale, is, that when you think about those foods, Coke is triggered in your mind. Another smart company named their cat food, meow mix. Therefore, whenever your cat cries meow, meow mix is triggered in your mind.

Emotion

Emotion explores the idea, that, **when we care, we share.** This involves crafting emotional stories around brands, so that as people share, they think about the brand as well. Here, Emotions are crafted as Trojan horses to carry brands. It is important to note that, not all emotions increase sharing. Some do, whilst others decrease it.

Public

Here, we exploit the idea, that, **when we see something, we are more likely to imitate it.** I observed something in my taxi rides in Ghana. I observed that usually, when one passenger pays the driver first, almost all the other passengers imitate too. Naturally, people are copycats.

Apple computers initially had their logos facing upside down, so that the user might know which side was up when taking it out of a bag. Therefore the logo appeared upside down to other people when the computer was in use. The manufacturer later flipped the logo, in order that other people might see it correctly, and imitate (i.e. buy Apple computers). Apple again introduced the white ear phone as a symbol of quality, making people imitate it.

Practical Value

This explores the idea, that, people share things because they have **useful content.** If you craft news people can use, they will surely share with others. Useful content may include *money/percentage off deals; 2 for 1 promos; travel deals; tit bits for healthy living etc.*

With money/percentage off deals, note **the rule of 100.** If something is less than $100, then percentage off seems better. And if it's more than $100, money off is better. For instance, it is better to promote $200 off a $2000 laptop, than promoting 10% off. Also, it is better to promote 20% off a $50 book, than promoting $4 off.

Stories

Stories thrive on the famous idea of the **Trojan horse.** Since people do not really believe in advertisement claims, narratives are proving to work. Stories deal with crafting useful information with a brand's benefit hidden inside it. People will share such stories not because they want to share your brand, but because they are sharing a useful story.

For more details on this strategy, read Jonah Berger's book, **Contagious – why things catch on.**

STRATEGY 2

VIRAL ADVANTAGE (VA)

The Viral Advantage is another approach to using viral ideas to project or sell a brand. There are two (2) kinds of Viral Advantage (VA):

* Automatic Viral Advantage (AVA)
  This involves seizing viral ideas created freely by other people just for making fun; and rather leveraging on their viral effect to project brands.

* Manual Viral Advantage (MVA)
  This involves consciously creating viral ideas, with the intention to leverage on their resultant viral effect to project brands. In order to launch an MVA campaign, a Viral Message (VM) must be crafted.

Not all ideas intended to go viral succeed. The viability or "virality" of a viral message depends on 3 things:

* Extraordinary Wit (creativity)
* Great Humor
* Relevance to time and place

If a message bears at least 2 of the characteristics above, any calculated campaign ridden on it will go viral.

Case study 1

In the later part of 2012, Ghana experienced a severe electricity problem, leading to a strict load shedding till the middle of 2013. During this time, a humorous message went viral on WhatsApp. Someone one had just crafted it to make fun. I seized the opportunity to propose an AVA for a client. Below is the viral message:

What good is it to own an LED TV, DVD player, 3 iphones, 2 ipads, 4 android phones, rice cooker, microwave, Jacuzzi, Air conditioner and have no electricity. Repent thy power is low.

I bet you would share this if you lived in Ghana at that time. And with Ghanaians being predominantly Christian, people could relate with the humour. The message was even funnier because of its relevance to the time and place.

Fortunately, I was working in an agency which had the **XYZ Generator** (Actual brand Name withheld) account. So, I proposed that since the message above had already gone viral, an Automatic Viral Advantage (AVA) campaign can be crafted.

On social media (Facebook, Twitter, WhatsApp) and SMS, I proposed the message below:

What good is it to own an LED TV, DVD player, 3 iphones, 2 ipads, 4 android phones, rice cooker, microwave, Jacuzzi, Air conditioner and have no electricity. Repent thy power is low; you need an XYZ generator *(actual brand name withheld)* ***today. Call 0244077783.***

On OOH/Outdoor (Billboards and Banners) I proposed the concept on the next page:

Case study 2

Agency was tasked to develop a mobile advertising campaign to support the Pepsodent **Cavity Fighter** campaign. As part of our ideas, we proposed a Manual Viral Advantage (MVA) Campaign for Facebook, Twitter, WhatApp and SMS. Therefore we crafted the Viral Message (VM) below:

- *If you want a pay raise, buy one or two zeros from your financial controller*
- *If you're struggling to cry, get more beatings*
- *But if you're struggling to fight your cavity, brush with Pepsodent only twice daily*
- *If you doubt, ask why every toothpaste in Ghana is called Pepsodent*
- *And if you want to help fight cavities, forward this message to only two people and one to shortcode **** for a handsome reward*

Whenever you think of going viral, consider any of these two (2) strategies above.

The Genesis of this Book...

One Simple Golden Question

ONE SIMPLE GOLDEN QUESTION

8

In March 2013, Ellie Jerow, a Digital Information specialist from Wisconsin, USA, posted a simple question on LinkedIn, the professional social media website. Her honest and direct question attracted the brightest, sincerest and generous people I have ever met in the world of Creative Advertising. For many days, Ellie's simple question generated a fun-filled and exciting discourse among renowned Copywriters, Art Directors, Creative Directors, as well as some Lecturers of Advertising.

During this virtual discussion, many creatives revealed the 'sacred and secret' books behind their success in the Creative Advertising industry. I was motivated to search and read 2 of the popular titles that surfaced; they were so captivating and 'page-turningly' irresistible. These books offered me complete education, and refreshing perspectives on Creative Advertising. You are about to read the awesome discussion that ensued, in a bid to answer Ellie's simple golden question, that:

"If you had to recommend one book to a beginning copywriter, what would it be?..."

Because of this simple question above, you are about to discover the secret of becoming the best in the advertising profession. Get excited!

JOIN THE DISCUSSION...

As indicated above, the following discussion/comments are based on this simple golden question –

"If you had to recommend one book to a beginning copywriter, what would it be? I'm looking for the best crash-course in effective copywriting out there. Would love your recommendations!"

Paul Dunwell
Copywriter and Project Manager
Guildford, United Kingdom

"War and Peace". There are too many would-be copywriters in circulation anyway. Hopefully, by the time you've read that, you'll have changed your mind.

Leanne Keough
Freelance Copywriter
Albany, New York Area

I would suggest "Hey Whipple, Squeeze This" by Luke Sullivan. It will help you grasp concepting, which often is a higher percentage of the job than the actual writing.

Renato Bratkovič
Managing & Creative director / Partner at Artizan, d.o.o.
Slovenia

- I would try Ogilvy On Advertising first. And Frederic Beigbeder's 99 Francs right after that. :)

Stacey Mathis
Owner at Stacey Mathis Copywriting
Greater New York City Area

If you had asked me two years ago, I would have suggested "The Adweek Copywriting Handbook" by Joseph Sugarman. But you're not. It's 2013. So, I'd recommend "The Idea Writers: Copywriting in a New Media and Marketing Era (Advertising Age) by Teressa Iezzi.

Ellie Jerow, MLIS
IA, UX, and organization geek
Greater Milwaukee Area

Well as much as I can appreciate what you're trying to say, Paul, it's already part of my job and I'd rather not fake my way through it. Do you have anything else you'd recommend?

Joe Ditzel [LION]
Ditzel & Company- Marketing and Copywriting | Copywriter | Marketing Consultant | Content Marketing | B2B Marketing
Greater Los Angeles Area

Can't pick one haha. Try:

Tested Advertising ~ Caples (4th Edition is best)
How to Write a Good Advertisement ~ Vic Schwab
How to Write Sales Letters That Sell ~ Drayton Bird
The Robert Collier Letter Book ~ Robert Collier
Break-Through Advertising ~ Eugene M. Schwartz
Influence The Psychology of Persuasion ~ Robert Cialdini
The Adweek Copywriting Handbook ~ Joe Sugarman

In writing good advertising, it is necessary to put a mood into words and to transfer that mood to the reader.

Helen Woodward

Tim Hearn
Owner at Tim Hearn Creative
London, United Kingdom

- I thought Hey Whipple, Squeeze This was as good as any that I've read.

Amruta Dhavale
Student at IES Management College
Mumbai Area, India

- Hey Whipple, Squeeze This by Luke Sullivan..... Definitely!

Michael Herbert
Copywriter at Marketecture
Manchester, United Kingdom

- Get 'The Copy Book'. It's a D&AD publication, full of brilliant, award-winning copy from some of the world's best writers. It never fails to inspire me when I take a look at it.

Richard Stoney
Experienced, award-winning copywriter
London, United Kingdom

- The best advice about writing copy isn't about writing copy.
  This piece of brilliance is by Andrew Rutherford,
  via D&AD Copy Book, via Dave Trott's Blog:

He bashed a knife loudly against a tin tray. Bang! Bang! Bang!...The din cut through the rowdy street market, and heads swiveled towards it.
"Ever tried to cut yer froat wiv a blunt knife?" he shouted, sawing at his jugular

with mock frustration. An interested crowd started to gather.

(Hint 1: Get attention. An invisible ad is not an effective ad)

"Better still, ladies. Ever tried to cut yer old man's froat wiv a blunt knife?" The laughter attracted more people. What's going on here? This might be fun.

(Hint 2: Intrigue your reader. But not irrelevantly. Lead him or her in the right direction.)

"I'll tell yer wot is murder ladies. Have you ever tried to cut the rind off a rasher, or fillet a fish, or string runner beans wiv a knife like this?" I started to lose interest and was about to move off when I noticed that several of the women were nodding in recollection. He'd struck a chord. I stuck around.

(Hint 3: Single out your target. Understand their problems, hopes and needs. Ignore everyone else.)

He scornfully flung aside the knife, and produced his "Little Miracle" as he called it. It looked just like a knife to me, but apparently it was like no other knife we'd ever seen.
He told us it was as sharp after 6 months of non-stop demonstrations as the day he'd discovered it. "Watch this," he said. And for the next few minutes with impressive dexterity, he sliced beans, sharpened a pencil, peeled an avocado, chopped a prawn...even shaved a slice from a stone.

(Hint 4: Always demonstrate your product's superiority if you possibly can.)

As he worked, he talked. He told us that the metal was discovered through space research, that micro-surgeons used especially fine scalpels made from it, and that this "little Miracle" (he wouldn't call it a knife) was banned from general sale in some countries, because it was "too easy to cut yer old man's froat wiv it".

(Hint 5: Facts are more persuasive than empty claims. But a little sugar can sweeten the pill.)

He told us we were lucky to be standing there, because the only other place he knew where we'd find it "was at 'arrods, where it cost ten quid. No tell a lie, £9.99 – 'arrods give you back up back from a tenner."

(Hint 6: Create a desire – a shortage perhaps.
Hint 7: Give the product credibility, Harrods in this case.)

However, he would save us the inconvenience of going all the way to Harrods. And better still he'd give us more than one penny back. In fact, he'd give us more than one pound back. How much? Five pound? No he was daft, but it was his nipper's birthday party, he was in a hurry to get away...so just this once he'd give us eight pounds back from a ten pound note. Just £2 for this "Little Miracle", but he only had a few, so...
A sea of hands shot towards him wildly waving banknotes to catch his eye.

(Hint 8: Clinch the sale. Make the buyer want to do something, and make him do it.)

As I walked away clutching my Little Miracle I began to sense that I had a lot to learn about persuasive selling, and that any aspiring copywriter could do a lot worse than go into the streets and watch a real pro like this at work.

Really, really great advice. And captivatingly written.

Pete Van Bloem
VP, Group Copy Supervisor at Draftfcb
Greater New York City Area

- The Book of Gossage is insightful and thoughtful, much like the most effective advertising ideas. Wish you well in your quest for a crash course.

The secret of all true persuasion is to induce the person to persuade himself.

Harry Overstreet

Conor Phillips
Marketing IBM in Ireland
Ireland

- Anything by drayton bird is worth a look. The man is brilliant!

Les Raebel
Kreative Chefin and Consultant at Raebel Kreative Werke
Greater Detroit Area

- The Copy WorkShop Workbook, by Bruce Bendinger. Gives a brief history of advertising along with writing instruction for all Media.

Jeremy Jaso
Creative at Sullivan Higdon & Sink
Wichita, Kansas Area

- Like Leanne said, more than half the job is concepting. I know teachers who use Concept and Copy in their college classrooms, so definitely pick that up if you haven't read it. I thought The Idea Writers was a good read on the current state of copywriting, but you probably won't learn much from it that you'll be able to apply to your 9-5. The Copy Book, Copy Workshop and Hey, Whipple are all on my bookshelf, and I'd recommend adding them to yours (note: The Copy Book is expensive). Other worthwhile reads include A Whack on the Side of the Head and The Creative Process Illustrated. Hope that helps.

Creativity can solve almost any problem.

George Lois

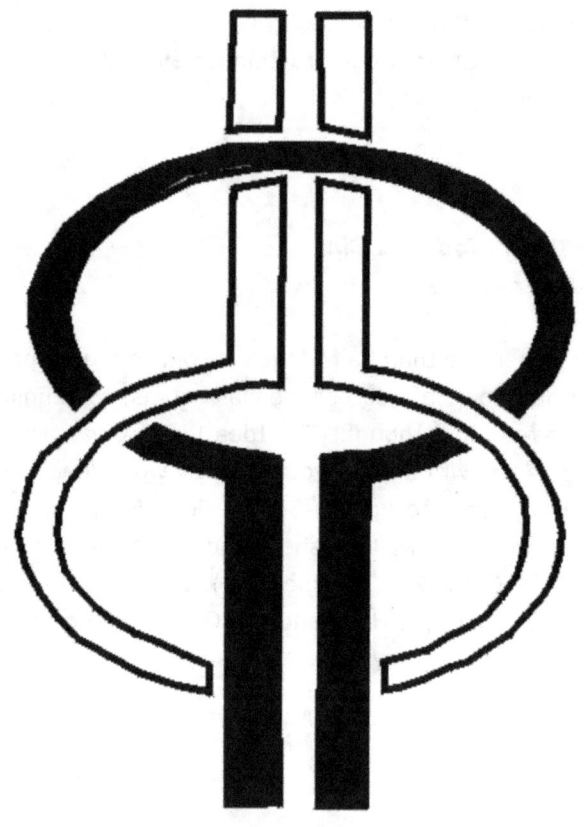

Shelley Jacobson
Copywriter at "The Creative Crew"
Ontario, Canada

- If you're new to the game and need a step-by-step guide on how to write copy for different mediums, check out: The Copywriter's Handbook by Robert W. Bly

A classic read on advertising is: Ogilvy On Advertising

I'm also a big fan of Seth Godin:
Check out "The Big Moo" Stop Trying to Be Perfect and Start Being Remarkable

Hope this helps.
Best of luck!

LeAnn Wilson McGuire
Owner/Pres/Creative Director at WilsonMcGuire Creative
Greensboro/Winston-Salem, North Carolina Area

- I'm going a little old school, but I'd recommend "What's the Big Idea" by George Lois and "From those Wonderful People Who Brought You Pearl Harbor" by Jerry Della Famina. Also, "Romancing the Brand" by David Martin. These guys are masters at idea making and writing. "Baked In" by Alex Bogusky & John Winsor isn't bad either -- but that's more about building products with a selling point baked into them than actually FINDING the selling point. Either way, they'll all inspire you! Any reading makes us better writers!

David Dutton
Sr. Copywriter/Account Manager at The Scott & Miller Group and Marketing and Advertising Consultant
Saginaw, Michigan Area

- "Broadcast Copywriting" by Peter Orlik was my Bible starting out and has been updated and expanded a few times now. "Ogilvy on Advertising" is a can't miss, too.

Cynthia Mejías
Freelance Creative Development and Translation
Puerto Rico

- The classic 'A Technique For Producing Ideas'.
  Another classic, 'Creative Whack Pack' comes in book form and as a card deck. It's basically an illustrated list of ways to approach idea production from unique perspectives

John V. Tremblay
Your mother always said you'd meet Mr. Write someday.
Greater Boston Area

- Dr. Frank Luntz's WORDS THAT WORK is outstanding. It's not focused exclusively on copywriting or advertising but any field (including politics) where semantics, brevity, and texture are required to engage your audience. I think sometimes we, as writers, get a bit flowery in our writing and this book reminds you how powerful a thoughtful, efficient word or phrase can be in moving someone. Practical, real-world examples from all walks of life. Especially useful if you're writing for digital or marketing. Highly recommended.

Advertising begins and ends with copy – begins with good copy, ends with bad.

Walter Weir

ADVERTYZENG

Jeff Sawyer
Group Creative Director, Brand Editorial at Lands' End
Madison, Wisconsin Area

- As mentioned above, "Hey Whipple, Squeeze This" by Luke Sullivan.

Jeffrey D. Wolff
Owner at The Thought Process
Greater Boston Area

- Probably all good suggestions but won't help if you don't know how to think... to think in a way that sets you apart from your peers and does away with so much of the By The Numbers Thinking that stifles good great ideas from emerging and suffocates them when they do. Here's an example I used before I hired any writer-------
Imagine a tiny duckling at the bottom of a milk bottle. The duckling is 50% larger than the mouth of the bottle and expanding the bottle via heat won't help. So... How do you get the duckling out of the bottle without damaging the bottle or the duckling? THINK !
And before you call me an Ahole, I worked for Bob Levenson, Gene Case and turned down offers from McCabe, Della Femina, Chiat, and finally George Lois, 3x.
One more thing...if copywriting is going to be rooted in SEO, where it now finds

Robert A.B. Sawyer
Partner at Limbo St. Marks LLC
Greater New York City Area

- I would recommend my own book: KISS & SELL: Writing for Advertising, because it was written specifically for "beginning copywriters" and is predicated on the counterintuitive notion that you can't teach copywriting.

Copy is a direct conversation with the consumer.

Shirley Polykoff

Instead, it introduces the notion of thinking, of using ideas/concepts as your starting point, and then discusses the uses of language. Then, to help you put it all in perspective, the book illustrates the ideas with 100 actual ads, largely picked at random.

Take a look: http://www.amazon.com/Kiss-Sell-Advertising-RedesignedRekissed/dp/2940373469/ref=sr_1_1?s=books&ie=UTF8&qid=1361909457&sr=1-1&keywords=kiss+%26+sell+writing+for+advertising+redesigned+and+rekissed Or you can find the Spanish edition on other sites.

Glenn Bossik
Sole Proprietorship at Glenn Bossik
West Palm Beach, Florida Area

- I'd recommend the book, Ogilvy on Advertising. In it, David Ogilvy gives a comprehensive overview of direct response copywriting, which is the driving force behind great advertising

Jeremy Feldman
Associate Creative Director at Atmosphere Proximity
Greater New York City Area

- I agree with "Hey, Whipple, Squeeze This." And, if you ever get to see Luke Sullivan speak in person, he's one of the most worthwhile and inspirational ad guys out there. As for the classics, I wholeheartedly recommend "When Advertising Tried Harder," a book about the advertising revolution in the 1960s with tons of examples of classic and great ads and campaigns that continue to influence advertising today. It's an entire advertising education in one well written, relatively short book, and you'll come away from it more savvy about the business.

The other great source, of course, are the ad award annuals, in particular those for the One Show, the Art Directors Club and CA (maybe D&AD as well). If you can find a collection of these, sitting down and going through, say, the past ten years gives you a really strong idea about where the state of copywriting is today. (I had a copywriting friend years ago who kept a notebook that contained all his favorite advertising headlines—whenever he was stuck for an idea, he'd leaf through the notebook for inspiration.)

Ken Lavery
Director of Marketing Saint Mary's College - Notre Dame, Indiana
South Bend, Indiana Area

* "When Advertising Tried Harder" by Larry Dobrow

  "Hitting the Sweet Spot" by Lisa Fortini-Bampbell

  "Crazy from the Heat" by David Lee Roth ;-)

Herb Bass
Senior Copywriter/Creative Director...web content, advertising,
marketing communications, executive speechwriting
San Francisco Bay Area

* Two books I couldn't get quickly enough when they were first published, back in the day, that is, are "What's the Big Idea" by George Lois and "From those Wonderful People Who Brought You Pearl Harbor" by Jerry Della Famina.

  "Ogilvy on Advertising" is also a must-read.

  I taught Advertising and Copywriting for a few years in the early-mid 2000's, and "Hey Whipple, Squeeze This" by Luke Sullivan was required reading as part of the curriculum

Resist the usual.

Raymond Rubicam

Robert A.B. Sawyer
Partner at Limbo St. Marks LLC
Greater New York City Area

- I'm not sure how to answer without appearing as a writer scorned, but here goes: I suspect one reason for the tsunami of bad writing, derivative writing and writing that comes across as a private joke is that people who have entered the business in, say, the last decade have read the books listed above, but read them out of context of time, place, and the simple economics at work.

  Yes, of course, read them. But read them with the same critical eye and ear as you would a biology text written before Darwin or a psychology text before Freud discovered the unconscious, or physics before Einstein or Hawkins, or prose before Joyce/Pynchon...you get the idea.

  Yes, read everything from the Bible through Shakespeare, to Emily Dickinson and Charles Simic, and, yes, this includes other ads, even for products that don't tempt you. Read all short forms of text, and don't neglect the caption of THE NEW YORKER comics (Illustrations.) Read the THE NEW YORK POST regularly and the TIMES on rare occasion. And, for God's sake, eavesdrop at every opportunity. Engage in gossip, even hostile, pointless gossip—not with much frequency, but you'll learn what flatters and what hurts. Toward that end, attend theater as often as you can afford and go to the movies on Friday afternoon.

  I've read or glanced at most of the books listed above and many more before writing KISS &SELL. And, I've met a number of the creatives, from Ogilvy and Frankfurt, to Lois, McCabe and Chiat; I've had long conversations with Steve Hayden and Bob Greenberg, and I can promise you that, like filmmaking, much of the creative process ends up on the cutting room floor. (Film? Cutting room floor? Take notice just how dated my metaphors are. Which is to say things are not as neat in life as they appear in heavily edited books.

  Two years ago, I had a contract to write a book on the future of advertising.

(Contract cancelled for a number of reasons) During that period I interviewed 20 or more of the industry's leading lights and talked about their campaigns that litter the One Show Annual and collect the 100s of glittering prizes that have turned Award Shows into Job Fairs. My conclusion: Great advertising is created in a fashion no different than any other highly collaborative art or craft.

Learn the fundamentals, learn to think critically and listen carefully, hope for talented partners and generous bosses, and learn to pray, too. Also, keep in mind that in today's world, if you don't attend SVA or Atlanta Portfolio Center or Miami Ad School, or you don't have a friend with some influence or powerful connections, you might consider going to a small city and look for work at a local agency, because it's highly unlikely you're going to find work in New York City. Unless, of course, you hang your own shingle (damn those archaic metaphors) and step out on your own.

Garrett Donaldson
Communications Director at JKR Advertising & Marketing
Orlando, Florida Area

- Jeffry's comment is spot on.

  The only other title I'd add to the ones mentioned throughout the string is Advertising Pure and Simple by Hank Sieden. Amacom – 1977

Daniela Kuper
Advertising & Marketing-Freelance
Greater Denver Area

- Skip the guerrilla-ninja stuff and grab "The Faith of a Writer: Life, Craft, Art" by Joyce Carol Oates. It'll feed your work and that secret project you haven't told anyone about.

Modern customers are so wild because of overexposure; it takes the successful copywriter to "catch them, and tame them"

Maxwell Ofori Nkrumah

Jan van der Reis
I help companies to generate NEW Leads for their business. Lead Generation and Marketing Strategy
Querétaro Area, Mexico

- These are resources I find valuable:
  John Carlton's "Kick-Ass Copywriting Secrets of a Marketing Rebel"
  http://www.marketingrebel.com/copywriting-salesmanship-closing-the-deal/john-carlton-kick-ass-copywriting/
  John Anghelache - The Copywriting Crash Course
  http://www.thecopywritingcrashcourse.com/

  Dan Kennedy Magnetic Marketing
  https://dankennedy.com/gkicsales/magneticmarketing.html

  And of course the works of Gary Halbert (The Prince of Print)
  Gary Halbert
  http://www.thegaryhalbertletter.com/http://halbertising.com/halbert-brothers-ad-breakdown-series-volume-1-jay-abraham-3/
  Hope this helps . . .

Carl Corbitt
Creative Director at Goodness Mfg.
Greater Los Angeles Area

- Hey Whipple, Squeeze This + The Book of Gossage + It's Not How Good You Are, It's How Good You Want to Be by Paul Arden. And as many award show books and CA advertising annuals you can get your hands on.

Alenka Zapušek
Copywriter
Slovenia

- Good observation, deep understanding and brilliant imagination. And then maybe a book.

Suzanne Lynch-McKay
Owner and freelance copywriter at Highland Tonic
Croydon, United Kingdom

- Another vote for Hey Whipple here.

Emily Suess
Marketing Communications Copywriter & Editor
Indianapolis, Indiana Area

- I have to put in another vote for Hey Whipple, Squeeze This by Luke Sullivan too. Although, Paul might have a point!

Maxwell Nkrumah
Copywriter at Admedia DraftFCB
Accra, Ghana

- These pieces remind me of the central idea in "The Copywriter's Handbook", by Robert W. Bly, that, "A Copywriter is a Salesperson behind a typewriter"

Maxwell Nkrumah
Copywriter at Admedia DraftFCB
Accra, Ghana

- I recommend "I have an Idea", by Akpo Daniyan

Sean Kirby
Senior Copywriter at Krames StayWell
Greater Philadelphia Area

- Tested Advertising Methods by John Caples is essential reading for any copywriter, but especially for a beginning copywriter. Though it's an oldie, it's a quick, easy read filled with examples. And it covers the basics like headline writing.

Garrett Donaldson
Communications Director at JKR Advertising & Marketing
Orlando, Florida Area

- "If you have any young friends who aspire to become writers, the second greatest favor you can do them is to present them with copies of The Elements of Style. The first greatest, of course, is to shoot them now, while they're happy." Dorothy Parker

LeAnn Wilson McGuire
Owner/Pres/Creative Director at Wilson McGuire Creative
Greensboro/Winston-Salem, North Carolina Area

- You might also consider whether you really want to WRITE or whether you want to come up with IDEAS. There's a big difference. Writing has changed in this field. I wrote a short blog about it: bit.ly/vnjiUM

Peter Dobbyn
Creative Intern at Rothco
Ireland

- I am reading 'Hey Whipple, Squeeze This' at the moment. It's proving to be a very insightful read.

Creativity is contagious, pass it on.

Albert Einstein

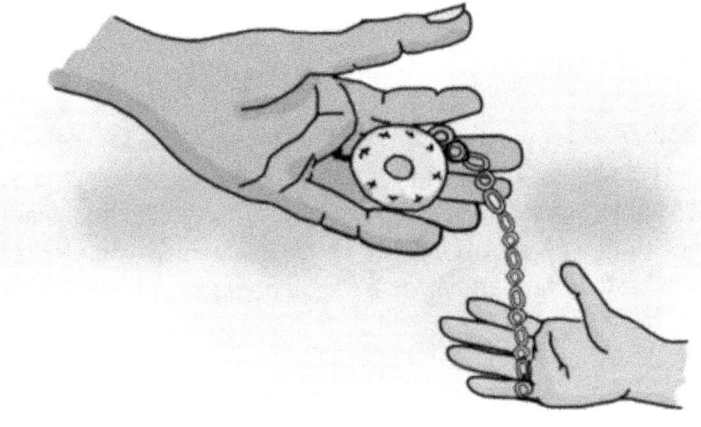

1st Copy BOOK for Advertising Copywriters & "Creative Writers"

TIM JACOBS
Principal at Bricolage Online Advertising
Toronto, Canada Area

- Echoing everyone under the sun here: Ogilvy's Confessions of an Advertising Man is a great book. Hopkins's Scientific Advertising is great too--and only a buck on Amazon (atrociously edited, though).

  After that I have to agree with Paul on Tolstoy. Tolstoy's What is Art? is indispensable, but then dip into Dostoevsky thereafter . . . If you don't read then you'll never be any kind of real writer, regardless of genre.

TIM JACOBS
Principal at Bricolage Online Advertising
Toronto, Canada Area

- Alright one more: go spend three months with David Foster Wallace's Infinite Jest. So many voices in your head--helps you understand the infinite variety of human experience. True art, totally authentic and real. Some of the finest writing I've ever seen. Read real stuff: everything else is just a list of tips. Understand human beings first, then you can refine techniques and strategies.

Joe Ditzel [LION]
Ditzel & Company- Marketing and Copywriting | Copywriter | Marketing Consultant | Content Marketing | B2B Marketing
Greater Los Angeles Area

- @Stephen Monday I show "Web Copy That Sells" is by Maria Veloso, not Angela Booth?

*If you're creative, you're not mad;
you only make people go crazy*

Maxwell Ofori Nkrumah

Patrick Kearns
Creative Director at AREA203
Chattanooga, Tennessee Area

- It's been mentioned Ad infinitum, the D&AD Copy Book is a must have. Also remember that writing is maybe 3% of the gig, the other 97% is a blend of concepting, head slamming, self deprecating, and screwing around. To that point I'd recommend A Technique for Producing Ideas by James Webb Young & The Internet is a Playground by David Thorne. Good luck.

Robert A.B. Sawyer
Partner at Limbo St. Marks LLC
Greater New York City Area

- My final contribution on this thread before saying au revoir:
  "The Bedroom Philosophers" by D.A.F. De Sade, because if you hope to succeed in copywriting/advertising, it's best you learn to anticipate, fear, and relish, submitting to and administering pain, pleasure, punishment and death

Marco Contardi
Copywriter, web editor, blogger & free writer
Milan Area, Italy

- Definetely "99 francs" by Frédéric Beigbeder... or is it too shocking?

Paul McQuillan
Direct Mail and Advertising Specialist
Greater Minneapolis-St. Paul Area

- Crash course? Don't see much of that listed. You want something that defines the marketing aspect of writing copy as well as writing the copy itself. I like books that have some entertainment factor while teaching. I would say for a beginner- Cashvertising by Drew Eric Whitman. I would follow that up with something to unleash the inner creativity with - POP! by Sam Horn

Atif Shaikh
Copy Supervisor at CNBC TV18
Mumbai Area, India

- Hey Whipple, Squeeze This - by Luke Sullivan...

Rachel Baron
Copywriter, Creative Consultant
Greater Chicago Area

- Here's a quote I share every single semester with my students. It's from Fairfax M. Cone, a former Chairman of Foote, Cone & Belding. In these few hundred words are the essentials a good copywriter needs to know: (and from here, I cut and paste :)

The plain, short story of good advertising

Advertising is the business, or the art, if you please, of telling someone something that should be important to him. It is a substitute for talking to someone.

It is the primary requirement of advertising to be clear—clear as to exactly what the proposition is.

If it isn't clear, and clear at a glance or a whisper, very few people will take the time or the effort to try to figure it out.

The second essential of advertising is that what must be clear must also be

Oga, Advertising is not a Joke. Advertising is a serious business.

Wale Adewale Adeoye-Famosa

1st Copy BOOK for Advertising Copywriters & "Creative Writers"

important. The proposition must have value.

Third, the proposition (the promise) that is both clear and important must also have a personal appeal. It should be beamed at its logical prospects; no one else matters.

Fourth, the distinction in good advertising expresses the personality of the advertisers, for a promise is only as good as its maker.

Finally, a good advertisement demands action. It asks for an order, or it exacts a mental pledge.

Altogether, these things define a desirable advertisement as one that will command attention but never be offensive.

It will be reasonable, but never dull.
It will be original, but never self-conscious.
It will be imaginative, but never misleading.
And because of what it is and what it is not, a properly prepared advertisement will always be convincing and it will make people act.

This, incidentally, is all that I know about advertising.

Xavier Roca Sancho
Publicitario
Alacant Area, Spain

- I'd recommend two books. Both books are focusing in how to think in advertising also, "The craft of copywriting" by Alastair Crompton, and "The advertising concept book" by Pete Barry.

Discovery consists in seeing what everyone else has seen and thinking what no one else has thought.

Albert Szent-Gyorgyi

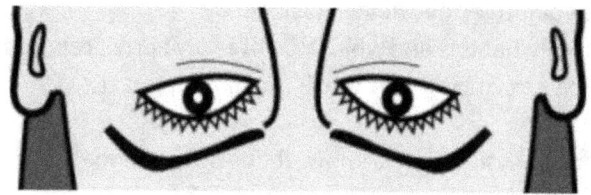

Mark Foster
Experienced freelance copywriter
Swindon, United Kingdom

- "Can I change your mind?" by Lindsay Camp. Great read.
  (That's a pint you owe me, Lindsay)

Roberto A. Ruiz Flores
Group Creative Director en Wunderman
Naucalpan de Juárez Area, Mexico

- Copy writing is about creating great stories where there is only a product and
  a target. I'll recommend the best Storytellers and the great stories: The Old
  Man and the Sea (Hemingway), The Great Gatsby (Fitzgerald), Casa Tomada
  (Cortázar), Rayuela (Cortázar). Then, I'll recommend ad books.

Daniel Escamilla
Advertising Art Direction Student
Greater Chicago Area

- One more vote for Hey Whipple + read the small but great book How to Get
  Ideas by Jack Foster. I could not recommend one without the other.

Jim Slattery
Writer and creative consultant
London, United Kingdom

- "From those wonderful people who gave you Pearl Harbour." Jerry Della
  Femina. It's a great read in its own right, irrespective of what it's talking
  about, which is what everybody forgets about good advertising copy.

Jeffrey D. Wolff
Owner at The Thought Process
Greater Boston Area

- Tim Jacobs is dead on. But I find it interesting that not one person has attempted to solve the riddle of the "duckling in the milk bottle" I laid out last week. I don't know if you all find it nonsensical or just don't want to risk your ego. No matter. Patrick Kearns gets in
the same arena with his comments, however unintentional.

Aditi Joshi
Copywriter I Educator I Editor I Blogger
Mumbai Area, India

- I would suggest Hey Whipple Squeeze This or The copy book or The Last Word...

TIM JACOBS
Principal at Bricolage Online Advertising
Toronto, Canada Area

- Well, it's not often I hear that I'm "dead on," so thank you, Jeffrey. (Came at a nice time, too, as I lost a juicy account yesterday. Boo-hoo).

TIM JACOBS
Principal at Bricolage Online Advertising
Toronto, Canada Area

- Maybe going slightly astray here, but to pick up on Jeffrey's comment about SEO and copy not going together, I have to say that that is bang on. Keywords are horseshit (can I say that here?) as is much emperor's-new-clothes SEO (time for a new thread, as it were?). Strong critical thinking and knowing who you're writing for and why ensures that you're covering the beloved keywords. Pumping keywords into content cannot make the content better. There is no calculus for innovation or a five step method for coming up with ideas. You've either trained yourself to think (to learn how to learn) your whole life or you haven't. Still, I have enjoyed the book suggestions by members here and have pounced on a couple that I hadn't heard of, perhaps to my shame. Sorry in advance if I've come off as harsh here. (The duck riddle is making my head hurt. . .)

Jeffrey D. Wolff
Owner at The Thought Process
Greater Boston Area

- You get the duckling out the same way you got it in...........
  Imagine!

Jeremy Johnson
Marketing and Strategy Wordsmith
Greater Salt Lake City Area

- Scientific Advertising by Claude Hopkins got me started, which lead to Ogilvy on Advertising and a slew of other books. I read shampoo bottles if I can't find anything else to read.

Sunil Shibad
Copywriter/Creative Director The Flea
Mumbai Area, India

1. Bill Bernbach's Book: A History of Advertising That Changed the History of Advertising by Bob Levenson.

2. Ogilvy on Advertising by David Ogilvy.
3. The Copy Book by British D&AD
4. Hey, Whipple, Squeeze This: The Classic Guide to Creating Great Ads by Luke Sullivan
5. It's Not How Good You Are, It's How Good You Want to Be by Paul Arden
6. What's The Big Idea by George Lois.
7. Scientific Advertising by Claude Hopkins

Rocío Carrillo
Web Editor Coordinator /Copywriter/Especialista SEO en Lomas Travel
Mérida Area, Mexico

- "The Copywriter's Handbook. Bly, Robert W. Third Edition." For me it´s the best

Ellie Jerow, MLIS
IA, UX, and organization geek
Greater Milwaukee Area

- Wow... so much good advice! Thanks so much, everyone! I picked a couple titles that seem to be popular picks to start off with, but will surely return to this thread for further reading once I'm done with those, as well.

  Really appreciate your willingness to take a few minutes and get me a push in the right direction. Thank you!

Bart Cleveland
Bart Cleveland Creative
Austin, Texas Area

- I love Luke Sullivan's "Whipple." I use it as a reboot continuously. Also consider, "The Idea Writers" by Teressa Iezzi. But I think writing advice outside of ad-focused books you can find great advice that will keep your perspective fresh. "The Mind of Your Story" by Lisa Lenard-Cook comes to mind as well as "The First Five Pages" by Noah Lukeman. So, I'm curious. Why do you need a crash course?

Lawrence Mannino
Senior Writer and Brand Strategist at LGM creative, LLC
Greater New York City Area

- I'd throw in The Adweek Copywriting Handbook by Joe Sugarman - especially if you want to get a handle on the direct response mindset - tough to find just one comprehensive one as 'copywriting' is pretty broad - if your read, say, The Idea Writers, you'll get a sense of copywriter as idea provider/ developer in a larger sense, which is good, while some of the other books focus largely on technique and triggers - all depends on your audience - hope you like to read ;)

Bruce Johnson
Marketing Consultant
Toledo, Ohio Area

- I suggest the same book David Ogilvy recommended in 1976. SCIENTIFIC ADVERTISING by Claude Hopkins; Foreword by David Ogilvy. Visit my website at bwjohnson999.wix.com/jim2 for comments on the sad state of advertising today.

Stephanus Angelo
Ad Operation Executive at Neo@Ogilvy
Sydney Area, Australia

- Start with these two books:

1. Ogilvy on Advertising by David Ogilvy and
2. Hey, Whipple, Squeeze This: The Classic Guide to Creating Great Ads by Luke Sullivan.

Samanta Llaguno
Marketing en Gaudena
Mexico City Area, Mexico

- uff you made my year of reading! thks to all for sharing

Anindya Banerjee
Branch Manager and Executive Creative Director at Scarecrow Asia
New Delhi Area, India

- The Copy Book is the bible for all advertising copywriters, past, present and future. Most books on advertising are brilliantly written but are about the copywriting process. My experience has been, nothing turns on students more than the final product. If they like the product, they will hopefully, become better students of advertising. (Rough analogy: make them love a Lamborghini before you try and turn them into auto engineers.)

Stan Obi
Creative Director at Potters
Nigeria

- What can copy writing do in branding?

Grace M McMahon
Copywriter. Creative. Writer.
Cape Town Area, South Africa

- 'Hey Whipple Squeeze This' by Luke Sullivan. It's my copy bible!

Melissa Pepers
Graphic Designer
Melbourne Area, Australia

- Got a few new books coming my way now!

I know you said one, but these four have been truly invaluable:
- Influence, the Psychology of Persuasion
- The Chicago Manual of Style
- Words that Sell
- Phrases that Sell

The first doesn't tell you what to write or how to write at all, it explores how persuasion works. As this is the aim of writing copy, Influence makes for a powerful resource.

Simon Aronowitz
The Testimonial Guru
Harrow, United Kingdom

- The Ultimate Sales Letter - Dan Kennedy

Demetrius Hill
Associate Creative Director - Copywriter at UniWorld Group
Greater Atlanta Area

- The dictionary

DD Kullman
Senior Copywriter at Off Madison Ave
Phoenix, Arizona Area

- I teach copywriting at The Art Institute of Phoenix. I'd definitely recommend "Hey Whipple, Squeeze This" by Luke Sullivan. Also "The Copy Workshop Workbook" by Bruce Bendinger.

Adam Kaplan
Creative Director. Leading creative for stronger brands.
Greater New York City Area

- Reality in Advertising by Rosser Reeves. It was written in 1961 and demonstrates how critical the USP is in your communications (they call that 'benefit' now). Honestly, it may be the only book you need.

Lana Winter-Hébert
Art Director, Writer, Editor
Quebec, Canada

- I'll put in another vote for "Hey Whipple, Squeeze This", and keep a copy of the Chicago Manual of Style within arm's reach.

Tom Stevens
Creative Director, Writer/Producer, Social/Digital/Mobile
Greater Detroit Area

- Ogilvy on advertising, for sure. Keep people glued and they'll read and buy.

Everyone has a genius; I call mine, the Holy Spirit.

Maxwell Ofori Nkrumah

SEVEN AUTHORS WHO
WERE COPYWRITERS FIRST

Signing Out

Let me conclude this book with a very useful insight which will further inspire you. With the exception of Paul Arden, being my personal contribution here, all write-ups on the other Six authors are credited to Nate Hopper; an American-based Freelance Copywriter.

For many writers struggling for publication, advertising has proven a useful field: **F. Scott Fitzgerald, Salman Rushdie, Dorothy Sayers, Don DeLillo, Joseph Heller and Helen Gurley Brown** all worked as copywriters early in their careers—some with more success than others. Rushdie came up with *"Naughty. But nice"* cream cakes for Ogilvy & Mather; Sayers introduced *"Just think what Toucan do"* to Guinness and founded a dotty, fictional (and wildly popular) "Mustard Club"; and, thanks to Fitzgerald, streetcars in Iowa once ran with the promise *"We keep you clean in Muscatine"* sparkling on their sides.

To these Creatives, advertising wasn't a waste of time: as Copywriters, some learned how to write economically and on deadline; others discovered fertile subjects in the office life and business culture around them; while others used office hours to work on the books that would later make their names.

F. SCOTT FITZGERALD

In February 1919, a 22-year-old F. Scott Fitzgerald was discharged from the army. He was without a job, but in love with a woman from Alabama named Zelda Sayre who refused to accept his marriage proposals until either a job or money materialized. So Fitzgerald moved to New York City in search of a newspaper position that would help him enter the writing world. In a fascinating 1935 interview with *The New York Post,* he described making the rounds of the newsrooms with a bundle of his lyrics for the Princeton Triangle Club, a theatre troupe, under his arm: "The office boys were not impressed." After a slew of rejections, he met a man who told him to skip out on journalism and invited him to come work as a copywriter for an ad agency.

Fitzgerald wrote short stories at night and, during the day, streetcar sign slogans for $35 a week. (Andre Le Vot's F. Scott Fitzgerald: A Biography mentions that

Fitzgerald also wrote lines for billboards—but fails to say if one was ever for a doctor.) "The hit I made with a slogan," he said in the Post interview, "I wrote for the Muscatine Steam laundry in Muscatine, Iowa—'We keep you clean in Muscatine.' I got a raise for that. 'It's perhaps a bit imaginative,' said the boss, 'but still it's plain that there's a future for you in this business. Pretty soon this office won't be big enough to hold you.'"

The pay was too meager to fund the lifestyle (and gin) Fitzgerald craved, and he'd soon pinned 122 rejection slips from magazines around his apartment. His distance from Zelda tortured him, too. So after only a few months, he quit copywriting—and New York City.

He later wrote: "I was haunted always by my other life—my drab room in the Bronx, my square foot of the subway, my fixation upon the day's letter from Alabama—would it come and what would it say?—my shabby suits, my poverty, and love. While my friends were launching decently into life I had muscled my inadequate bark into midstream... I was a failure—mediocre at advertising work and unable to get started as a writer. Hating the city, I got roaring, weeping drunk on my last penny and went home."

At his parents' home in St. Paul, Fitzgerald reworked a novel he'd written during the war about a young Princeton student who'd enlisted, expanding the book to include the student's post-war struggles in New York. It was titled This Side of Paradise, and in March 1920, thanks to some in-house championing by Maxwell Perkins, Charles Scribner's Sons published it. While the book didn't net Fitzgerald much money, it popularized his work and allowed him to charge more for his short stories. It also made him suitable for marriage. A day after the first printing sold out—three days after its release—Fitzgerald wrote to Zelda, asking her to meet him in New York City and marry him. She did.

SALMAN RUSHDIE

One day, in 1969, Salman Rushdie ran into a former acquaintance who'd disappeared from the London fringe theatre scene in which Rushdie was active. "He'd bought a sports car, he had a blonde secretary and he was making shampoo commercials with tall thin girls. He also looked like he had put on a considerable amount of weight," Rushdie said in an entertaining guest speech for a 2008 advertising-awards ceremony. "He said, 'You should try this, Salman, because it's really easy.'"

Rushdie went to take a test at the large agency, JW Thompson, where the man worked. "The only question I remember was they asked you to imagine that you met a Martian who mysteriously spoke English and you had to explain to them in less than 100 words how to make toast." (D.C.R.A. Goonetilleke's biography mentions that the test also asked for a jingle on the merits of seatbelts.) He failed the test.

Rushdie snagged a copywriting position at a smaller firm but then quit to finish his first novel, **The Book of the Pir.** But when the book didn't find a publisher, he began working a couple afternoons a week at then-"relentlessly unfashionable" Ogilvy & Mather, dividing his time between copywriting and writing. "As I look back, I feel a touch of pride at my younger self's dedication to literature, which gave him the strength of mind to resist the blandishments of the enemies of promise," he wrote later. "The sirens of ad-land sang sweetly and seductively, but I thought of Odysseus lashing himself to the mast of his ship, and somehow stayed on course."

Rushdie was not the only aspiring author at the agency, of course, and he describes his colleagues hiding their manuscripts and screenplays in their desks whenever the agency's head would fly in from New York. His seven years at Ogilvy & Mather were productive. For the **Daily Mirror,** he came up with, "Look into the **Mirror** tomorrow—you'll like what you see." He also thought up "Naughty. But nice." for a cream cakes company after watching a bunch of Brit sitcoms (the line's an allusion to Dick Emery's "You are awful (but I like you)"). The client initially rejected the concept, but a year later, without Rushdie's foreknowledge, the tagline was everywhere, including TV:

There was also "Irresistibubble" for Aero, which remains the candy-bar company's slogan today. Aero wasn't Rushdie's account, but a panicked, blocked coworker asked him to help brainstorm. The coworker was so nervous as they batted around ideas that he was sweaty and stammering. Then, as Rushdie remembered it in that same 2008 speech, the man was on the phone and his stutter kicked in: "Whatever he was asked he said he couldn't do," recalled Rushdie. "He said, 'It's impossib-ib-ib-ible', and I thought, 'Ping!' It was one of the very few ping moments actually. While he was still on the phone sweating and stammering I wrote down every word I could think of that ended with 'able' or 'ible' and turned it into 'bubble'."

Throughout his time as a copywriter—including a switch to Ayer Barker, where he came up with the tagline, "That'll do nicely," for American Express—Rushdie kept writing. While at Ogilvy & Mather, his first published book, **Grimus,** was released. At Ayer Barker, he wrote his next novel; one morning, he spent a couple office hours deliberating over what to call it, typing "Children of Midnight" and "Midnight's Children" over and over at his desk before settling on the latter.

Rushdie left copywriting in 1980, the year before **Midnight's Children** was published, but never lost the habits he'd formed as a copywriter: "I now write exactly like that. I write like a job. I sit down in the morning and I do it. And I don't miss deadlines. I do feel that a lot of the professional craft of writing is something I learnt from those years in advertising and I'll always be grateful for it."

DOROTHY SAYERS

In a 1922 letter to her parents, Dorothy Sayers wrote, "I've no idea whether I shall make anything of this business." She was in London, in the midst of a month-long trial period at the advertising agency Benson's. Her letters from this period are filled with fretting over whether she'd get cut from the job, which paid four pounds a week, a salary she needed to supplement earnings from **Whose Body?,** the first of her Lord Peter Wimsey mysteries.

But Sayers was brought on permanently and landed a raise and an office to herself on the agency's top floor. She relished the creativity and the word play of the job, notes James Brabazon in his biography. When she went out to pubs with her coworkers she'd wear a lapel badge of the Froth Blowers, the beer drinkers' union.

Sayers wrote ads for a number of sandwich ingredients, including Sailor Savouries, margarine and mustard. In another letter to her parents, in 1923, she wrote: "Mustard again! It is astonishing that they should want so many advertisements for mustard. However, let's hope that's the end of it for a bit."

It wasn't, though. The creation of the Mustard Club—one of the most popular ad campaigns of the time—occupied her time for the next few years. Hatched from an inside joke between Sayers and her future husband, journalist Atherton Fleming, the club was described in one ad this way:

The Mustard Club (1926) has been founded under the Presidency of the Baron de Beef, of Porterhouse College, Cambridge. It is a Sporting Club, because its members are always there for the meat. It is a Political Club, because members find that a liberal use of Mustard saves labour in digestion and is conservative of health. It is a Card Club, but Members are only allowed to play for small steaks. The motto of the Mustard Club is 'Mustard Makyth Methuselahs,' because Mustard keeps the digestion young. The Password of the Mustard Club is *'Pass the Mustard, please!'*

While Sayers was never formally acknowledged as the campaign's chief copywriter, Brabazon observes that the entire campaign had Sayers' touch: from its fictional characters (Miss Di Gester, the secretary; Lord Bacon of Cookham, among others); to a prospectus that claimed the club had been founded by Aesculapius, the god of medicine; to the recipe book, which included a Shakespeare and Chaucer reference by a "Devilled beef" recipe: "Who sups on a devil should have Mustard in his spoon." The fictional club grew so popular it issued roughly a half-million real memberships before the war.

The agency's offices had an iron spiral staircase, and Brabazon describes Sayers descending the stairs, her cloak waving behind her, a cigarette holder in one hand and the other hand in the pocket of a black jacket or holding scribbled concepts. One frequent destination was the office of illustrator John Gilroy, with whom Sayers worked, in 1928, on the famous zoo adds for Guinness. The collection of these ads on the Guinness website says the campaign didn't debut until the mid-'30s, after Sayers' tenure at Benson's; and according to the Guinness Collectors Club, Gilroy continued producing Guinness ads into the '60s, using the same themes. But Sayers is widely credited for her work on the concept and the original jingle: "If he can say as you can/Guinness is good for you/How grand to be a Toucan/Just think what Toucan do."

In 1930, Sayers would leave the agency to pursue her writing full-time. By then she'd published five mysteries and a collection of short stories. In 1933, she used her memories of the place to speedily come up with the premise for a mystery in order to hit a deadline (she later hated the book because of how rushed its writing was). The book, **Murder Must Advertise,** was centered around the mysterious death of a copywriter who falls down an iron spiral staircase. Lord Wimsey, going undercover at the agency to solve the case, finds that he has a surprising knack for copywriting and comes up with a successful campaign for Whifflet cigarettes. Gazing into a mirror one day, Wimsey remarks, "Strange, to think that a whole Whifflets campaign seethes and burgeons behind this solid ivory brow."

Don DeLillo

Like Rushdie, Don DeLillo worked at Ogilvy & Mather (although in the New York, not the London, offices). But, unlike Rushdie, DeLillo is not to be found giving fond speeches at advertising-awards ceremonies. In a 1991 New York Times interview, DeLillo said he'd only taken a job as a copywriter after he couldn't turn up one in publishing. After working at the agency for five years, he quit and, as he put it, "embarked on my life, my real life." But the transition away from writing print ads (he never worked in commercials) wasn't so he could write, he'd later tell Guernica: "Actually, I quit my job so I could go to the movies on weekday afternoons."

DeLillo has steadily maintained that "his experience as an advertising writer… explain[s] little in his career," notes Thomas Pietro in the introduction to his compilation **Conversations with Don DeLillo.** Yet traces of the experience can be found in his novels. As Mark Osteen, president of the Don DeLillo Society, wrote in an email: "Most of this experience fed into his work—and particularly into his first novel, **Americana,**"—which DeLillo began writing three years after leaving Ogilvy—;"in which the character Clinton Bell, is an adman… A lot of what [DeLillo] has to say about it comes in Clinton's words: for example, that 'television is an electronic form of packaging.'"

In **Americana,** Clinton tells his son David, the novel's protagonist, a story about a shrewd piece of marketing devised by his own father: "McHenry—the Star-Spangled Pajamas," pajamas with 48 stars sewn on every pair. The product made the company owner rich and Clinton's father famous. "It was the greatest merchandising gimmick of the decade," says Clinton before concluding, "You could afford to be innocent in the days."

In another scene, David asks his father, "Why is it that all advertising people I've ever known want to get out? They all want to build their own schooners, plank by plank, and sail to the Tasman Sea. I know a copywriter at Creighton Insko Dale. At lunch one day he started to cry."

JOSEPH HELLER

In 1953, Joseph Heller was working as a copywriter for the Merrill Anderson Company in New York. One night, as he later described it to The Paris Review, "this line came to me: 'It was love at first sight. The first time he saw the chaplain, Someone fell madly in love with him.'" As he remembered in his autobiography Now and Then, he sat down at his desk that day and wrote an entire chapter longhand.

Two years later, the chapter, entitled, "Catch-18," was published in **New World Writing** (in the same issue, a chapter from Kerouac's **On the Road** was published under the pseudonym Jean-Louis). Heller made $25. By then he'd left the agency and a couple other jobs and was working as an advertising-promotion copywriter at **Time.** In his new biography of Heller, Just One Catch, Tracy Daugherty recounts how Heller once successfully wooed the Simmons mattress company to buy ad space in Time by using an image of the Red Queen from an old edition of **Through the Looking Glass** and the quote, "Now, here, you see, it takes all the running you can do to keep in the same place!" in a presentation—a success that got him his first raise.

Another two years passed and the chapter had become a halfway-finished novel with a publishing contract. Another four years, during which Heller moved to **McCall's** as a promotions manager, and the book was finished and released under the new title: **Catch 22.** Another two years and the novel was the bestselling paperback of the year, selling over two million copies; but only earning its author $.03-$.04 a copy, by Heller's own math. (That's about half a million in today's dollars.)

It wasn't until a year-and-a-half later, when the movie rights were sold for $100,000 (that'd be about seven times that today), that Heller left the advertising world.

HELEN GURLEY BROWN

Helen Gurley Brown was 31 and an agency secretary when she won a 1953 *Glamour* magazine competition to share the title of "Girl with Taste." The victory brought her a trip to Hawaii, minor celebrity status and, eventually, a shot at a promotion to copywriter. Although it's not clear that a career in copywriting was even Brown's true goal—what she really wanted was to win the contest. "I felt I better not say I just want to be a secretary, that wasn't what they were looking for, so I said **'I'd like to write copy,'**" she later recalled. But then, as Jennifer Scanlon recounts in Bad Girls Go Everywhere, a staffer from *Glamour* called up Brown's boss and asked him why he hadn't given her the opportunity to write copy, his wife seconded the question and Brown got her chance.

Brown ferried back and forth between her secretarial desk and her copywriting desk for three years. Apparently, her boss found it hard to replace her (he'd later say that was the real reason he hadn't promoted her earlier). The agency was Foote, Cone & Belding, and while there Brown wrote lines for Sunkist, Catalina swimsuits, Breast-O'-Chicken tuna and Lockheed, among other accounts.

But her flair for writing copy that appealed to women garnered such high demand that another agency successfully lured Brown away with an offer of twice the money. For Max Factor eye makeup, she wrote: "It's nice to be an angel most of the time—but tonight—let your eyes reveal the daredevil side of you! Let them go deep, dark and devilish...suggesting, just suggesting the wanton and wicked." For Max Factor's Pan-Cake line: "Tonight you must be more beautiful than you really are... you must be beautiful, period, when your mirror has been telling you for years that the most extravagant adjective that can ever apply to you is...attractive. Poof to that! Tonight you will be beautiful!" Within a decade Brown was the highest paid copywriter on the West Coast and had won several awards for her work.

Throughout her time working as a copywriter, she sent in advice articles for women to *Glamour, Playboy,* and *Esquire,* without success. But then came the bestselling *Sex and the Single Girl* in 1962, and Brown said "Poof to that!" to the ad world when she took over as editor-in-chief of *Cosmopolitan* three years later.

PAUL ARDEN

Here's how Roger Kennedy described Paul Arden:

"Brilliant, bad, charming, irascible and totally off the wall. An original with extraordinary drive and energy, blessed with a creative genius allied to a kind of common sense that just isn't, well, common."

As Executive Creative Director at Saatchi & Saatchi during its heyday, Arden was responsible for some of the great campaigns of British advertising, including British Airways and Silk Cut. But he is also remembered as one of the great characters of the industry.

Arden's unconventional management style is legendary. When a piece of work failed to meet his exacting standards, it was not unknown for him to express his displeasure by jumping up and down on it. Yet the majority of those who worked with him cite his great passion and unyielding perfectionism as utterly inspirational. Even after stepping down from his full-time agency career, Arden continued to devote time to helping students and young creatives.

In 1993 Arden set up the film production company Arden Sutherland-Dodd. In his latter years, as well as opening a photography gallery, Arden and Anstruther, in Petworth, Sussex, he developed a highly successful second career as a writer. A weekly column in The Independent was followed by the publication of his first book, ***It's Not How Good You Are, It's How Good You Want To be,*** which sold over half a million copies. This was followed by two more titles, ***Whatever You Think, Think The Opposite*** in 2006; and the last being, ***God Explained In A Taxi Ride.***

For a creative synopsis of his book, "whatever you think, think the opposite", visit www.funandjoyatwork.com/images/Think-the-opposite.pdf

ABOUT ME

After earning my BFA in Theater Arts and Music from the University of Ghana, only one thing was certain to me - success. But there were several jobs on my mind, partly because, I believed I could fit into so many positions due to the interdisciplinary nature of the performing arts.

I started as Social Studies teacher for a Junior High School; then after University, a part-time Sales Agent for a telecoms company ; proceeding to teaching English Language in a Senior High school; and finally, an Advertising Copywriter.

I got into Copywriting as a result of curiosity and passion for advertising. Television commercials and Billboard advertisements fascinated me. I craved to be part of this world of advertising. Now I'm stuck here, and addicted to Copywriting. The only job I may do aside Copywriting, is, perhaps being a Lecturer. Probably, teach Copywriting. I love this job! It feels good to get paid for your imagination.

Through professional experience, Copywriting is now like a hobby to me, since I've grown not to struggle at it. I'm currently the Head of Copy at Admedia DraftFCB, Accra-Ghana.

Philosophically, I am an Idealist; I don't "rationalize too much". Optimism is my attitude to life; and consciously, I live on the positive side of life. Because, really; life is good and beautiful.

BIBLIOGRAPHY/WEB SOURCES

- **The Decision Book**
  Fifty Models For Strategic Thinking by Mikael Krogerus and Roman Tschäppeler

- **Contagious –** why things catch on by Jonah Berger

- **The tipping Point** by Malcolm Gladwell

- **The copywriter's Handbook**
  A Step-by-step guide to writing copy that sells by Robert W. Bly

- **The New Rules of Viral Marketing**
  How word-of-mouth spreads your ideas for free by David Meerman Scot

- **Whatever You Think, Think The Opposite** by Paul Arden

- **I have an Idea** by Akpo Daniyan

- **Hey, Whipple, Squeeze This**
  A Guide to Creating Great Ads by Luke Sullivan

- **A Technique for Getting Ideas** by James Wood Young

- **Scientific Advertising** by Claude C. Hopkins

- **Advertising Strategy:**
  Creative Tactics From the Outside/In by Tom Altstiel and Jean Grow

- www.brainstorming.co.uk

- www.skymark.com

- www.wikipedia.com

- www.theawl.com/2011/08/six-authors-who-were-copywriters-first?goback=.gde_58585_member_271443059#!